CONTENTS

T0058912

INTRODUCTION

Your drumming experience has included big bands, combos, Latin bands, concert and marching bands, commercial parties, and weddings. Does all this experience prepare you to be a show drummer? Not really. Having played in all these different contexts definitely enhances your ability to play drums, but in order to play shows—musicals, variety shows, TV shows, and so on—there are specific skills you must learn. The purpose of this book is to explain these skills and how best to utilize them. Whether you play shows professionally or as a school project, the tools you need to get started are in these pages.

The Purpose of this Book/CD

We created this book/CD package to address the "missing elements" in most drum methods—namely, those that apply to show drumming. It is our intention to provide an in-depth treatment of all the rhythms needed for shows. You will find examples of tangos, waltzes, and many other rhythms that are generally missing in the inexperienced drummer's repertoire. For the most part, our book focuses on the "big three" styles of drum set playing—rock, jazz, and Latin music—but the ethnic and country/western rhythms we have included are also important. Next to knowing these rhythms, the "how" of playing them is important. Listening and learning to play show and ethnic music, as well as rock, jazz, and Latin, is essential. There is a great feeling of satisfaction that comes from knowing and playing this wide variety of show beats. The drummer who "covers it all" is a valued commodity to leaders and conductors in our business.

This book is divided into two parts:

1. The practical, "how-to" information and lessons

2. A hypothetical show that puts you in the position of the show drummer, with CD accompaniment and step-by-step instruction from Ed

A Note from the Conductor

My responsibility as a conductor is to have complete knowledge of the artist's music and the ability to communicate all its details clearly, quickly, and with courteous control. Very frequently I have had only one hour to "talk over" a show—this means only verbal discussion and little or no playing. This can create a lot of tension and apprehension for the orchestra, the artist, and obviously myself. However, if I know the drummer has show experience, can sightread well, and has a cooperative attitude, I can move forward quickly and with confidence. Every instrumentalist in the orchestra is important, but the drummer is the vital rhythmic artery that makes the show flow—or clogs it up and gives everyone a heart attack.

When I started conducting, my extensive experience as a drummer was a tremendous asset. I remembered all the great conductors whom I admired and always tried to emulate their styles.

SHOWDRUMMING

THE ESSENTIAL GUIDE TO PLAYING DRUMSET FOR LIVE SHOWS AND MUSICALS

CD INCLUDED

Percussion photos courtesy of LATIN PERCUSSION.

ISBN 0-634-06823-7

HAL•LEONARD®
CORPORATION
7777 W. BLUEMOUND RD. P.O. BOX 13819 MILWAUKEE, WI 53213

In Australia Contact:
Hal Leonard Australia Pty. Ltd.
22 Taunton Drive P.O. Box 5130
Cheltenham East, 3192 Victoria, Australia
Email: ausadmin@halleonard.com

Visit Hal Leonard Online at
www.halleonard.com

DEDICATION

We would like to dedicate our book to our wives, Ilene Shaughnessy and Shirley De Rosa, and thank them for their support and love.

ACKNOWLEDGMENTS

Special thanks to the following talented percussionists for their support, belief, and guidance: Sandy Feldstein, Jim Coffin, Joe LaBarbara, Joel Leach, Garwood Whaley, Richard De Rosa, Kent (Duke) Allman, Mark Dicciani, Justin Di Cioccio, and Dean Witten.

RECORDING CREDITS

Production:	Clem De Rosa and Ed Shaughnessy
Conductor:	Clem De Rosa
Engineer:	Mike Caudle–special kudos to this talented young man for his patience and cooperation
Recording Studio:	Citrus College, Glendora, CA
Music:	Clem and Richard De Rosa
Musician's Contractors:	Billy Kerr and Nancy Newman
Musicians:	Drums–Ed Shaughnessy
	Percussion–Gary De Rosa
	Saxophones–Billy Kerr, Ann Patterson, and Bruce Eskovitz
	Trumpets–John Thomas and Larry Williams
	Trombones–Les Benedict and Jim Burr
	Piano–David Arnay
	Bass–Chris Clarke

FOREWORD

In our many years together on the "Tonight Show," Ed Shaughnessy and I played over 5,000 acts. They ranged from the fields of pop, opera, rock, jazz, and Latin music, and included singers, dancers, jugglers, comedians, and impressionists. In all these situations, Ed was the ideal show drummer who handled the daily challenges with ease. He was dependable, positive, and helpful to me in every area.

Clem De Rosa has long been a pioneer in music education, as well as a fine drummer, arranger, bandleader, and conductor. He brings with him the combined knowledge of what the conductor needs from the experienced show drummer.

I know this fine combination of Ed's playing and lessons, the recorded musical examples, and Clem's combined conducting and drumming experience will serve greatly in providing information and guidance in a somewhat neglected, but truly important, field.

Enjoy and learn!

Doc Severinsen

My conducting responsibilities include:
- Making conducting patterns, cues, and tempo changes clear and definitive
- Communicating quickly and without incident any artistic surprises during the performance
- Being prepared to accept minor mistakes for a good finished product

What are some of the drummer's responsibilities?
- Arrive early to set up and be ready for rehearsal
- Look through the music quickly
- Mark and highlight all musical signs, time signatures, repeats, etc.
- Listen closely to the conductor as he/she talks over the show. If you have any questions, be clear and speak to the specific problem.
- Give constant attention to both the music and the conductor
- When the conductor stops the orchestra, stop playing and listen!
- Remember, your job is to play the music for the artist. Save your technique, speed, and fancy fills for your next Basie or Ellington gig.
- Remember also that the goal is to play the music well. It is a team effort with you and the conductor having the greatest responsibility to make it happen.

Ed and I address all of these issues in the following pages, and we hope that all the material in our book will guide you as you develop into a fine show drummer.

Clem De Rosa

ABOUT THE AUTHORS

Prior to his twenty-nine years with the Tonight Show band, **Ed Shaughnessy's** big-band and jazz experience gave him the skills and knowledge which he successfully adapted in his work with Doc Severinsen and the band. During those many years, Ed played over 5,000 different types of acts in every conceivable musical setting. He is a seven-time winner of "Best Big Band Drummer" in the *Modern Drummer* magazine poll, and *DownBeat* has called him "America's finest all-around drummer." Ed is also an inductee in the 2004 Percussion Hall of Fame. He has played on over 500 albums and done over 600 clinics.

Clem De Rosa's career as a drummer included big band, jazz, and show experience. In later years, Clem attended Juilliard and the Manhattan School of Music, earning a Masters Degree. During his twenty-six ensuing years as an educator and administrator, he remained focused on his conducting, arranging, and composing skills. He has led and conducted the Copacabana Show Orchestra and the orchestras of Glenn Miller, Jimmy Dorsey, the Dorsey Brothers, Tribute to Benny Goodman, and the Les Musique de Broadway Review, among others. In these musical settings he has conducted and/or arranged for vocalists, dancers, comedians, and instrumentalists. Co-founder and past president of the International Association of Jazz Education, Clem's honors include induction into the Jazz Hall of Fame in 1990, an honorary Doctorate of Education in 1992, and a gold record as co-producer (with Dave Grusin) of the Glenn Miller CD "In the Digital Mood."

Ed and Clem represent the two key musicians (drummer and conductor) who bear the major responsibility for the satisfactory performances of all the artists in a show setting. In this book, they share a pragmatic application of the skills necessary to be an accomplished show drummer.

DRUM KIT EQUIPMENT

This section lists all the essential equipment that you will need to bring with you to every show as part of your drum set. The following sizes and types of equipment are recommended to get the sounds that are most versatile and best support the band.

Bass Drum

Size:	14"x22" or 14"x20"
Heads:	Coated white with impact pad
Muffling:	Felt strip (2" wide) on each head, or sponge rubber piece on shell
Hardware:	Good spurs; firm mounts for tom-toms or cymbals
Foot Pedal:	Sturdy, with built-in spurs
Beater Ball:	Felt is best for shows

Tuning

Batter Head:	Medium tight
	(If playing a rock-based show, loosen the batter head a little)
Front Head:	Medium tight

Playing

Jazz:	Play lightly, except for accents
Fast Jazz:	Use short strokes
Rock:	Play strong

Snare Drum

Size:	5"x14" or 5 1/2"x14"
Shell:	Wood or metal
Heads:	Plastic
Top Head:	Coated white
Bottom Head:	Thin & clear
Snares:	16 wire strains

Tuning

Bottom Head:	Higher in pitch
Top Head:	Medium tight

Playing

Play in the center for a full, crisp sound
Play soft rolls near the edge, close to the rim

Tom-Toms

Size:	Rack toms: 8"x12" or 9"x13" (mounted on the bass drum)
Floor toms:	16"x16"

Tuning

Medium tension, top and bottom

Playing

Play in the center for a full sound

For practice, play patterns for the snare on the various tom-toms

Cymbals

Crash Cymbal:	16" medium thin, positioned on the left side
Ride Cymbal:	20" or 21" medium heavy
Alternate Ride:	18" medium pitch, positioned on the right (also good for cymbal rolls)
Other:	10" or 12" thin cymbal for choke sounds

Hi-Hats

Size:	14" top and bottom
Weight/Pitch:	Top: medium weight and pitch
	Bottom: heavier and lower in pitch
Pedal:	Sturdy with good height adjustment

Stands

Three floor stands, sturdy with a firm base

One cymbal holder mounted on the bass drum

Sticks and Beaters

Sticks:	5b or light stick 5a
Brushes:	Heavy and light with rubber covering
Mallets:	Hard and soft felt mallets for tom-tom and cymbal rolls
Alternate Mallets:	Wrap butt ends of sticks in moleskin for fast tom-tom and cymbal rolls without changing sticks. There are some manufactured sticks available which are a combination of stick and mallet.

Small Table

This is an essential item to include in your set for quick changes of sticks, brushes, mallets, etc. It should be covered with a towel or cloth so changes can be made quietly. The table should be placed within easy reach of the player, usually on the left.

Electronic Drums

There are many useful applications of electronic pads for musical sounds or special sound effects. (Yamaha and Roland are two leading companies in the field.) Knowledge of the use of a MIDI controller is also important.

Since these products are constantly being updated, we are not recommending specific units. All drummers should explore the wide range of information available on these products.

ACCESSORIES

In addition to the basic drum kit, a drummer should own and be able to play the following accessories:

Cowbell (C.B.)   **Triangle (Trgl)**   **Tambourine**

Maracas   **Claves**   **Woodblock (W.B.)**

Mallet instruments such as orchestra bells, vibraphone, xylophone, and chimes are more specialized, and most drummers will not be expected to be proficient on them. If there are extensive parts written for these instruments, an additional percussionist will be hired. However, a basic knowledge of these accessories, and the ability to play parts on them that are not too demanding, will certainly enhance your work opportunities.

Select accessories are explored in further detail in the pages to come. If you are not familiar with them already, you must become acquainted with them. Play them and listen to the different qualities of sound they produce. When you know their distinctive sounds, you can occasionally substitute a regular piece of drum set equipment that might be acceptable. For example:

- Use the wooden rim of the bass drum to simulate a woodblock

- Hit the cup of a cymbal with the metal handle of a brush to simulate a triangle

- Use large cymbals to simulate gong sounds

When you have no advance notice of any special accessories for rehearsal, you will have to make do with something that is reasonably close to the required sound. After the rehearsal, however, make every effort to get the correct accessories.

IMPORTANT: Often, conductors and arrangers will refer to these accessories as "toys." If you strike these percussion instruments too forcefully, the quality of sound will truly resemble that of a toy!

Cowbell

This accessory comes in many sizes and pitches, and is used primarily in Latin music. However, it can also be used for special sound effects. Most bells are designed for mounted use, but they also provide great muffled tones when handheld. The lower-pitched version tends to be somewhat larger. Accents are played on the edge of the bell.

Cowbells can be purchased with a forged eye-bolt assembly to provide a sure grip to any 3/8" diameter rod.

The Triangle

The triangle can lay claim to being one of the first purely metal percussion instruments to enter the modern orchestra. The instrument is a steel bar bent into the shape of an equilateral triangle, with one corner open. It is struck with a steel beater (sometimes tapered) or a wooden drumstick. The triangle is an instrument of indefinable pitch, as its numerous high dissonant partials obscure the fundamental note. The average triangle measures 6 1/2" to 7" per side and is made from hardened steel. Its construction permits a variety of tone colors.

The triangle is suspended by a thin string, preferably of gut. It is held in one hand or hung on a support and can be hit in several different places for a variety of tones. Generally the outer side, the apex, or the lower end of the closed side is preferred for quiet sounds. Strikers of various weights are also utilized for different sounds.

To observe note values, the fingers of the non-playing hand clasp the upper section of the instrument to dampen it at the appropriate moment. For the trill (roll), the beater is placed inside one of the closed corners of the instrument (the top or bottom), and the two sides are struck in rapid alternation, the crescendo being affected by moving the beater to a larger area within the triangle.

The player must exercise great care in tone production. Badly manipulated, the triangle will give the impression of a fire bell. In the hands of an artist, its sound can enhance the most delicate situation or reinforce the climax.

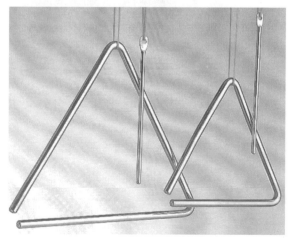

Tambourine

Structurally, the tambourine is a frame drum consisting of a wooden hoop with a single head (traditionally of calfskin). In the shallow wood shell are openings for the jingles, small metal discs held loosely in position by steel pins that pass through the center of each disc. The jingles are arranged in either one or two rows, and the head is usually nailed to the shell. The orchestral tambourine is commonly ten inches in diameter.

The tambourine is notated on the staff. Numerous ways of playing the tambourine allow the instrument a whole range of possibilities. Playing techniques include:

- Striking the head with the knuckles, fingertips, palm, or closed fist
- Shaking the instrument, causing only the jingles to sound a sustained note, trill, or roll

- Striking the rim with the fingertips of both hands or the drumsticks—in which case the instrument is placed on a soft-topped stand

- Playing by means of friction, i.e. rubbing the head with a moistened thumb to produce either a thumb roll or a given number of recurring strokes. In this case the moistened thumb is rubbed along the surface of the skin near the rim. The speed of the movement vibrates the jingles, controlling the number of "bounces" or notes. To assist in this technique, the calfskin, if not mounted with the coarser side on the exterior, is roughened or resin is applied.

Maracas

This accessory is used almost exclusively in Latin music. There are many sizes, either made with plastic shells or natural rawhide shells. Most are fitted with a steel-ball fill and all come in matched pairs. The round plastic design delivers a crisp sound while the rawhide shell has a drier but livelier sound. They are held in one hand (as shown) and typically shaken in an eighth-note pattern like this:

Claves

Claves are traditional instruments used to play *clave*, the rhythmic pattern that forms the basis of most Latin music. The two sticks are struck together for a sharp, cracking sound. One is called the clave, the other is the striker.

The clave lies in one hand between the fingertips and the heel of the hand, with the thumb out for support. The space between the clave and the palm of the hand creates a sound chamber. The striker is held in the other hand and struck against the clave. Each stick measures 10" x 1".

Woodblock

The woodblock is, as the name suggests, a rectangular block of hard wood, with a slotted resonating cavity. The tone of the orchestral woodblock is penetrating, and will surmount the heaviest *pf* orchestral tuttis. It is struck on the surface, over the slot, usually with a drumstick or xylophone beater. In works of lighter character, the woodblock serves a variety of sound effects, imitating a clog dance, the patter of horses' hooves, a knock on a door, or the comic sound of tapping on someone's head.

The woodblock has a holder and can usually be mounted on the rim of the bass drum. Even if not mounted, it will have an effective sound.

Temple Blocks

In contrast to the woodblock, which is usually used singularly, temple blocks are used in varying numbers, most often in pairs (high and low). In incidental music, these quaint-sounding instruments are used to suggest the color of the Orient. They are also called upon to supply many sound effects, from the popping of a champagne cork to the gurgling of a dripping water tap. In performance, they are laid on a flat pad or mounted, and struck with a rubber or hard felt beater.

Castanets

The castanets are usually made of ebony, rosewood, or a similar wood—or occasionally of a synthetic material. Although they're traditionally played by hand (the Spanish method), this was impractical for show drummers because of the need to make quick changes to other percussion instruments. An alternative is for a pair of shells to be mounted on a central handle (or a pair at each end of the handle). For a tremolo, the instrument is shaken in the air as a rattle, the shell beating against the central board. Rhythms are produced by striking the instrument on the knee or palm, or tapping the shells with the fingertips. A device known as a castanet machine is now frequently used.

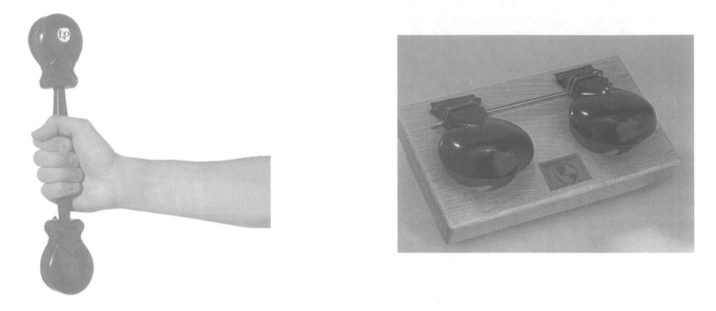

Wind Chimes

This very effective, light-sounding accessory is used for lightly scored compositions. It features 3/8" diameter aluminum alloy chimes of various lengths, strung with cord on a wooden holder.

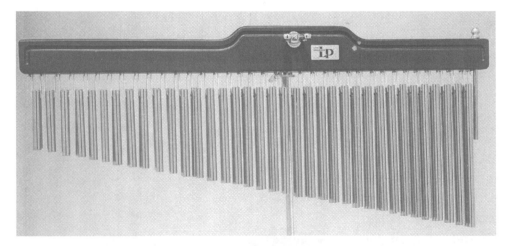

The wind chimes are played by sliding a small striker from the largest chime to the smallest, or vice versa. A drumstick can be used instead of the metal striker, if you don't have time to change.

Sleigh Bells

Sleigh bells are a series of small bells of unselect pitch attached to a strap, wire frame, or upright handle (as shown). Rhythms similar to those on the tambourine are given to jingles. The tremolo produced by shaking the instrument is particularly effective when augmenting a brilliantly colored tone scheme. For rhythmic patterns, the bells are tapped on the palm of the hand.

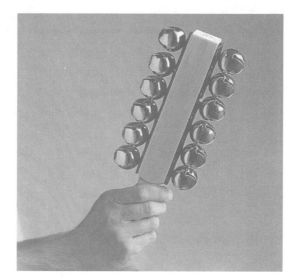

Orchestra Bells

The orchestra bells are comprised of a series of steel bars of graduated length, arranged chromatically in two rows; the back row is usually raised (à la the black keys on a piano). For maximum resonance, the bars are supported on felt or similar insulation, or suspended at the nodal points. The standard sets have a respective range of two and a half and three octaves, sounding two octaves higher than written in notation (treble clef). The mallets are of flexible cane shafts with several kinds of heads, including wood, bone, plastic, rubber, and even metal.

In rapid figures the pitches of the bells tend to overlap, but this characteristic of the instrument is rarely detrimental to the music.

The responsibility for playing this instrument usually falls on an auxiliary percussionist. However, your ability to play the instrument will enhance your opportunities to be hired.

MUSIC VOCABULARY

It is important to understand the many musical terms that are constantly being written on all musical parts; they should be part of your musical knowledge. Listed here are most of the terms you will encounter, their meanings, and their abbreviations. If you're an experienced music reader, you probably have seen many of these terms before. Make sure you have them down: you never know when an obscure but important term will show up on a piece of music.

Tempo Markings

A Tempo	Return to the previous tempo
L'istesso Tempo	Same tempo
Adagio	Slow
Alla Breve	Cut time (2/2)
Meno Mosso	Slower, literally "less motion"
Andante	Moderately slow, "walking" tempo
Maestoso	Slowly, majestically (with dignity)
Moderato (Mod.)	Medium tempo
Allegro	Fast
Accelerando (accel.)	Tempo becomes faster
Presto	Fast quickly
Ritardando (Rit.)	Gradually slower. Synonymous with Rall.
Rallentando (Rall.)	Gradually slower
Rubato	Freely (free time)
Piu Mosso	Move quickly, literally "more motion"
Poco a Poco	Little by little

Dynamics

Term	Symbol	Meaning
Pianissimo	*pp*	Extremely soft
Piano	*p*	Soft
Mezzo Piano	*mp*	Medium volume, literally "medium soft"
Fortissimo	*ff*	Very loud
Forte	*f*	Loud
Mezzo Forte	*mf*	Medium loud
Crescendo	*cres*	Increasing in volume
Pianoforte	*pf*	Soft, followed by crescendo
Sforzando	*sfz*	Strong attack and crescendo
Diminuendo	*dim*	Getting softer (decrescendo)

More Important Terms

Da Capo	*D.C.*	"From the top"—Return to the beginning
Dal Segno	𝄋	"From the sign"—Return to sign and repeat the music from there
Coda	⊕	Final section added to the regular form
Fermata	⌒	Pause or hold; let ring out
Cadenza		Improvised passage played freely
Cue (on cue)		Special entrance dictated by the leader
Non Troppo		Not too much
Pesante		Heavy
Reprise		Repeat of music played earlier
Segue		Move directly to the next section
Simile		Almost like, similar to (as on a repeated phrase)
Tacit		Be silent; don't play
Tutti		The full orchestra

Solo		Featuring one instrument
Soli		Featuring a section of the orchestra
Volti Subito	*V.S.*	Turn the page quickly
Double time		Tempo moves twice as fast
Double time Feel		4/4 meter stays, but the rhythm section plays twice as fast (as if in 2/2 time)
Cut off	*//*	Sudden stop; called "railroad tracks"
"Play the Ink"		Play part exactly as written
⬦∿∿∿⬦		Don't play the music in brackets
"Catch"		Terminology for drummers to accent a distinct movement or gesture by the artist
👓		Look carefully for an important cue
Tag		Short extension of the chart
Vamp		Repeat phrase until the cue to move on
Fine		The end

TIME, TEMPO, OR PULSE

This is the most vital element for the performance of any musical composition. The establishment of a pulse, and the ability to maintain that pulse from inception to completion, is essential. All of the musicians in an ensemble have a shared responsibility to attain this goal, but it is the drummer who has the power and the muscle to bring any wavering of the time back into its original slot. The conductor, because of his/her position in front of the orchestra, becomes the second most important person to correct any time problems. The two, working together, are the prime movers and controllers of the tempo.

Because show drumming usually involves several written time or tempo changes within one piece of music, the drummer must maintain the following:

- Absolute focus and mental awareness of what is happening musically
- The ability to adjust his/her playing to fit the style of music
- Frequent eye contact with the conductor for any tempo changes or special dynamic changes
- Choice of definitive rhythmic patterns to lock in the new tempo (lock in all tempo changes using a simple rhythmic pattern, and lock in with the bass and the conductor)
- Attention for any special effects to enhance the artist's performance

ENERGY, INTENSITY, AND VOLUME

Jazz

Energy, intensity, and volume: three words that cause confusion among drummers. You must learn to create energy and intensity without increasing volume. There are several levels of energy and intensity that drummers should learn and utilize. An exercise in building intensity in jazz follows.

Level 1   *p   mp   mf*

Practice keeping time at various tempos with just the ride cymbal, hi-hat, and bass drum. The strong beats 2 and 4 on the hi-hat (with your foot) and the same emphasis of this accent on the ride cymbal will create the first level of intensity. The bass drum should be played lightly to add some bottom to your sound—it should be felt more than heard. When you establish a balance between these pieces of equipment, the intensity and energy can be increased by a stronger accent on beats 2 and 4 on the ride and hi-hat. Total concentration should be on the balance and intensity of these three pieces, practiced at all tempi.

Level 2   *mf*

Using the left hand on the snare, with simple rhythmic patterns to support the ride cymbal, you can increase the level of intensity and help drive the band. Great care must be used with this device, however. Don't get too busy with your left hand, because it could distract from the basic time feel and musicality of the arrangement.

(Snare drum softer than cymbals)

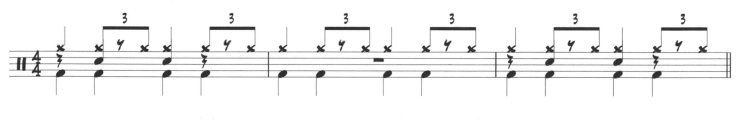

Level 3   *mf   f*

Continue with the three pieces of equipment used in level 1, and lay the left stick on the snare with 3–4" of the butt end extending past the rim. Strike the rim, making a "click" sound.

Play the left hand on the fourth beat of the measure to reinforce the accent of the ride cymbal and foot hi-hat. Because the foot hi-hat and the left hand do not increase the volume, you can increase the strength of your attack. This will create more intensity without getting louder.

Level 4   *f*

Using the same approach as level 3, you can add the left stick on beats 2 and 4 ♩ ♩ ♩ ♩. This will increase the intensity and energy.

Level 5   *f*

While maintaining the left stick on the rim (on beat 4 or beats 2 and 4), changing to another cymbal with a different pitch quality (higher or lower) will introduce another color and add a variety of intensity and volume (up or down).

Level 6   *ff*

Finally, the strongest pattern for *ff* (very loud) ensemble playing incorporates the left hand on the snare, playing a rim shot on 2 and 4 ♩ ♩ ♩ ♩.

The proximity of the left hand's striking distance to the snare head will determine the volume of your accents. When the ensemble has reached this volume, you need to use all the elements to maintain control of the tempo.

Rock

Level 1

Play eighth notes on closed hi-hats, and place the left stick partially on the snare and the rim. Play a "click" on beats 2 and 4 (lightly).

The bass drum pattern can be:

Level 2

Play the same pattern as above (at medium volume), but play 2 and 4 accents on the snare. The bass drum can play any pattern.

Level 3

Play strong eighth notes on the ride cymbal with equally strong snare beats on 2 and 4. The bass drum can play any pattern.

Additional Thoughts

It's always a challenge to keep the energy and intensity up while playing *pp* (very soft) passages. One approach for soft ensemble passages is to use the tip of the stick on closed hi-hats with a slight accent on beats 2 and 4. The bass is locking in the time, and you are adding the intensity and energy.

MORE TIPS

Accenting Performances

The show drummer learns early on that one of the most important aspects of the job is to keep the band together while accenting dance moves, magic tricks, and other critical moments of a performance. Here are some of the secrets to accomplishing this:

- Catch the acts with "hand sounds" while keeping time with your feet, for example:

ETC.

- Use the snare drum (with or without rim shots), tom-toms, and cymbals to give a variety of sounds

- If the bass drum is needed for accents, keep hi-hat time

- Cowbell, woodblock, and additional percussive accessories can add more color and variety

Foot Patterns

At fast tempos, this foot pattern works well:

The same pattern can work in rock style at slower tempos.

In 4/4 swing, this pattern works:

Roll Practice

It is rewarding to practice rolling while maintaining feet patterns:

Tips on Folding the Music

Since the drummer often keeps playing at page turns, it is very important that a quick one-handed page turn shows at least the next two pages of music. This is accomplished by an accordion-like folding of the music to reveal both pages:

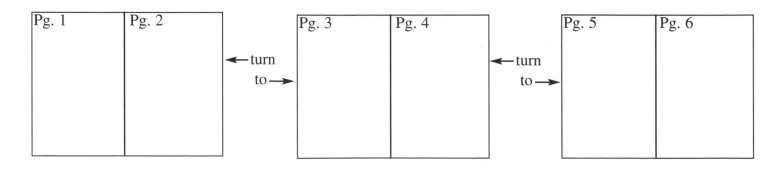

Exceptions

There are situations in which we depart from the two-page system. If we are soloing or rolling, using both hands at the time of a two-page turn, we must adjust to a single-page setup or a three-part section fold to eliminate the page turn while both hands are busy.

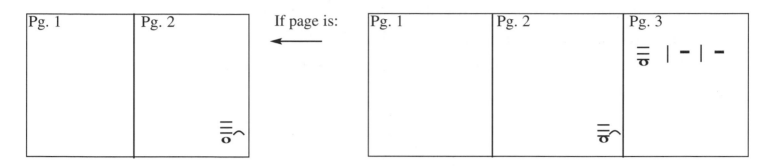

Music Stand Placement

Seeing the conductor is crucial when playing shows, but so is seeing your sheet music. Try the music stand positions recommended below.

Position A

Place the music stand over your hi-hats. This works best for left-handed page turns, and if the conductor is straight ahead or to your left.

Position B

Place the music stand over the far edge of the floor tom. This is used if the conductor and/or the acts are to your right (Ed's situation on the Tonight Show). Right-hand page turns are necessary, so be ready to "fake" the rhythm with your left hand.

NOTE: Many young drummers in school bands put their music stands in front of the bass drum, making it impossible to turn pages while playing. This might work in the jazz ensemble, but it will not work in show drumming. It is not really a good habit to develop!

RHYTHMS

Shuffles

A shuffle is best defined on the snare drum with the left hand  while the right hand plays the basic ride cymbal figure . If a lighter sound is required, then the shuffle on closed hi-hats or ride cymbal with the backbeat on the snare will suffice:

Strong Shuffle (fast tempo)

Bass drum plays quarter notes,
foot hi-hat plays on 2 and 4:

Medium Shuffle

This form uses a standard ride cymbal and bass drum figures as above, with the left hand on the snare playing the shuffle with accents on 2 and 4 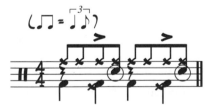.

Light Shuffle

The cross-stick rim "click" may be used
on the backbeat:

Very Light Shuffle

Use brushes on the snare:

Waltzes

Standard (Commercial)

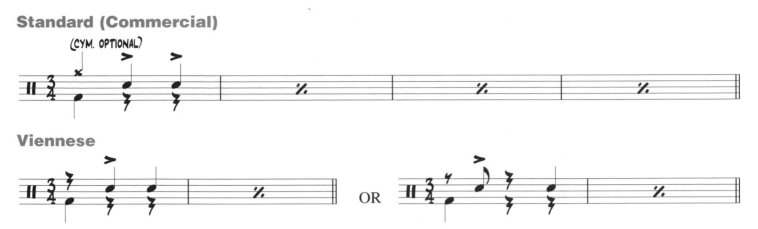

Viennese

OR

Jazz

If the bass is playing on the first beat of each 3/4 measure, then the drums play that feel on the bass drum, along with this cymbal rhythm (notice the foot hi-hat on beat 2):

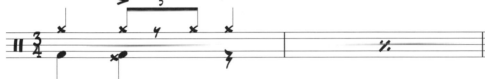

If the bass is playing all three beats in the measure, drums then shift to that feel on the bass drum:

Latin

🔊 Track 1

Ed demonstrates mambo, songo, samba, and more Latin beats (beguine, merengue, conga, and calypso) on track 1 of the CD.

Bossa Nova

This easy groove uses a continuous bass drum pattern combined with a clave-type rhythm in the left hand with a cross-stick rim sound. To get this sound, lay the left stick on the snare with 3–4 inches of the butt end extending past the rim. The main part of the hand lays on top of the stick, and the fingers lift the butt end to contact the rim:

Mambo

This is a spirited dance-type rhythm. Play this figure on the bell of the ride cymbal with the right hand (or a cowbell, if available). The left hand plays the cross-stick and tom-tom:

2:3 clave:

In a more workable mambo pattern, the bass drum plays a simple half-note rhythm (with hi-hat on 2 and 4): ♩ ♩ ♩ ♩ . If a 3:2 clave fits better, reverse the two measures.

Songo

Play a steady cowbell (or cymbal bell) rhythm, and a combination snare/bass drum pattern in the left hand (snares turned off):

Samba

This is a generally bright groove:

Other Ethnic Rhythms

Track 2

Ed demonstrates all of these ethnic rhythms on track 2.

Paso Doble in 3/4

Paso Doble is Spanish for "double time." It is helpful to "ghost" the downbeats (play lightly); this steadies the placement of the upbeats and the tempo:

Paso Doble in 2/4

Freilach (Jewish beat)

Played in a lively tempo:

Spanish Tango

The "other" tango—not to be confused with the Argentine tango on the CD!

Greek Rhythms

Kalamatianos

Karshilamas

Tsamikos

6/8 Rhythms

Italian Tarantella
Irish Dances
Mexican Hat Dance

All three can be approximated with this pattern:

SIGHTREADING

The ability to sightread at one hundred percent accuracy is the number one prerequisite for show drumming. Knowledge of the musical vocabulary is essential. Since shows necessitate many changes of tempo, time signature, and musical styles, the drummer must learn the skills to apply these elements when seeing the music for the first time.

Unlike other areas of music, there is not enough time for many repeated rehearsals of each show piece—thus the need for excellent sightreading and getting it right the first time.

Don't Get Lost

This is the cardinal rule for reading any music. It's always important, but even more so in show music, where the drummer most often sets the tempo for each new section. You must constantly be looking ahead for these tempo changes and be prepared to lock in the new tempo.

One of the best methods of practicing sightreading is to have plenty of new material As you search for new material to read, try reading the rhythmic patterns on trumpet, trombone, or saxophone parts, interpreting the figures as you keep time on the ride cymbal or hi-hat. Start by looking through various musical libraries and get permission to duplicate saxophone, trumpet, or trombone parts. Before you play, mark the long and short notes. Over time, you can eliminate this step and make a judgment as to the interpretation of the part without marking it. Remember to always play two or four measures of time (on the hi-hat or stick clicks) before starting to read the part.

Work on a new page or two at each practice session. Remember that once you start the page, *don't stop!* When you're playing the show, you won't have the luxury of stopping! This is the way you must practice. It means accepting a limited number of mistakes to gain the benefit of reading "the whole page."

Listen carefully to how the drum figures are played on the "Playing the Show" section of the CD. The time is always prevalent, and on any figures, Ed plays with the ensemble to reinforce the attack of the horns, never interfering with the flow of the music. On the Tonight Show, the band had only forty-five minutes to rehearse new music for all the guest artists. With such a limited time for rehearsal, accurate and musical sightreading was vital.

Long and Short Sounds

When sightreading, show drummers will often have only a horn chart to work from. It is up to them to be able to interpret this music in an accurate and efficient manner. By marking up the chart with specific symbols, the drummers can indicate to themselves where and when long and short notes and accents will occur in the music. The chart below shows convenient symbols to use for long and short sounds.

Long Sounds   (for the whole drum kit):

Rolls   (snare drum or tom-toms):

Short Sounds   (for the whole drum kit):

Snare	Struck with stick in the middle of the head (*mf*):	
Rim Shot	Struck with stick using snare head and rim (*ff*):	
Cymbals	Supported with the snare or bass drum playing simultaneously with the cymbal attack	
Choke Cymbal	Strike cymbal with right hand and quickly stop the ring with the left. Works best with a thin, smaller cymbal (10 in.).	
Hi-Hat	Played open-to-closed with the foot (a soft, short *mp* sound)	

The melodic line of the music will determine the horns' decision to play long or short notes. The drummer must interpret the part without this advantage, and make two decisions:

1. What notes in the figure will be long or short?

2. What pieces of the kit will best reinforce the horns and fit the texture of the music?

Here are some guidelines:

*   Look through the chart before you play it, and mark long and short notes using the symbols shown above

*   The final interpretation of the music will be determined by the structure of the melodic lines and the conductor's concept

At a moderate tempo, the execution of these long and short sounds will allow you a wide variety of equipment choices. However, another element to consider is the volume and texture of the music—low or high pitch quality; soft, medium, or loud. Because the melodic instruments are concerned with the horizontal flow and spin of the figures, the drummer must also play the figures with the same concept; e.g., long sounds sustained into the short sound. Here is an example:

Here is another example of long and short sounds, and how to play them:

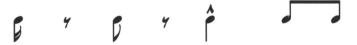

In this two-measure phrase, the ♪ is the point toward which the figure is spinning, and consequently it gets the strongest attack (but don't bang!). The short quarter note ♪ at the end puts a button on the figure. Thus, a crisp rimshot supports the horns' attack.

Interpretation of the written part, determining long and short sounds, will vary in different styles of music. With experience you'll learn to make the correct choice of instruments within the drum kit to produce the sounds that best fit the musical texture of the moment.

Long and Short in Jazz, Rock, and Latin

When playing figures in these styles, it is important to match the accents to the length of the figure at hand. Basically, there are two categories we observe:

Short sounds including the following are played on the snare drum:

Long sounds, including all tied notes, are played using a cymbal, supported with the bass drum to give the figure a more legato sound:

Figures that look like this on the page...

...are played like this:

This approach works well when playing these three styles—but remember, rock and Latin music traditionally have a straight-eighth feel, whereas jazz typically has a 12/8 feel.

Suggestions

When seeing the music for the first time

- Look for the musical signs that will be your guide as you play the chart, and highlight them with a red pencil: Dal Segno 𝄋; Coda ⊕ ; Repeats 𝄆////𝄇; Cutoffs (//); and so on

- Mark long and short sounds

- Mark sections of repeats with numbers (in red pencil):

This simple system helps you avoid the need to follow those repeated measures one by one, and makes for a more accurate method of maintaining your place on the chart. It also gives you the opportunity to make eye contact with the conductor.

Vital Accessories

- Two #2 pencils with erasers

- Two red pencils

Observing Rests

There are two ways of notating rests on drumset parts. The literal observance of silence usually occurs when rests are inside the staff:

If, however, the rhythms are written above the staff, we continue playing time and add the written figures:

This is especially true in show playing with tempo changes, fermatas, cut-offs, etc. The clear understanding of these two notations is critical. Occasionally, a written part will have rests in the measure, but when the drummer observes them , the conductor will say, "don't stop the rhythm there." In this case, simply write "keep rhythm" over those measures:

Sightreading Material

Saxophone, trumpet, and trombone parts are an excellent source of sightreading material. We have included some examples of horn parts that can be used for sightreading. The long (⁻) and short (∧) notes are indicated on the part. Also marked are the melodic lines that should be *tacit* ("not played"), because you don't want to interfere with the melodic flow of the moving parts (just play time).

Practicing Sightreading

- Mark long and short sounds before you start

- Play two or four measures of time (on the ride cymbal or hi-hats) before playing each exercise

- Repeat each exercise three times without stopping

- Practice at various tempos

- Each practice session can be a new sightreading experience by starting with different combinations of rehearsal letters. For example, play A–B–C, then C–A–B, then B–D–A, etc.

- Create your own new combinations of the written exercises, so you don't memorize the rhythms

- Don't try to play all the rhythmic figures as left-hand independence exercises; many exercises sound and feel better when played hand-to-hand or hand-to-foot

- Use a variety of the instruments on your set—snare, tom-toms, cymbal/snare, etc.—to match the texture and color of the music

- After you've played what we have written and created your own sightreading exercises, play the whole page with some ride cymbal or hi-hat time between each rehearsal letter

- Remember the cardinal rules: "**Don't stop**," and "**Keep the tempo locked in!**"

SIGHTREADING EXERCISES

Abbreviation Key

These abbreviations will be used in the sightreading exercises to follow:
(Refer to the Music Vocabulary section of the book for more help.)

L.S. (⌣)	Long Sound	Cym	Crash Cymbal
S.S. (∧)	Short Sound	B.D.	Bass Drum
S.D.	Snare Drum	L.H.	Left Hand
R.C.	Ride Cymbal	R.H.	Right Hand
R.S.	Rim Shot	C.B.	Cowbell

Drum Notation

For the sightreading exercises:

Ride Cymbal or Hi-Hats (closed) (H.H.)

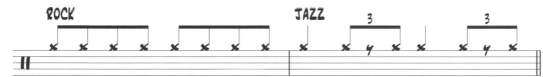

Foot Hi-Hats

Accessories (or "Toys")

Tom-Toms: Small (SM. T.T.)   **Medium**   **Large or Floor Tom (LG. T.T.)**

Snare Drum (S.D.)

Bass Drum (B.D.)

Sightreading Exercise #1

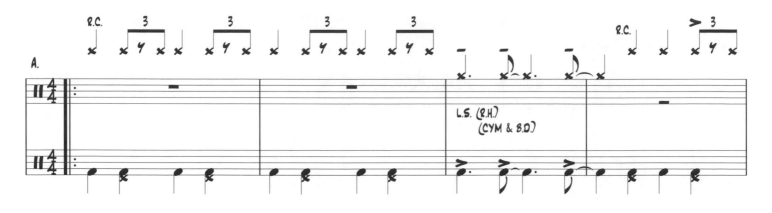

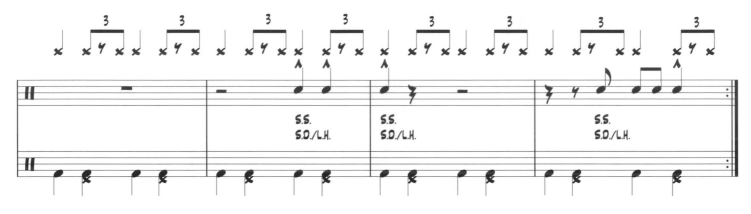

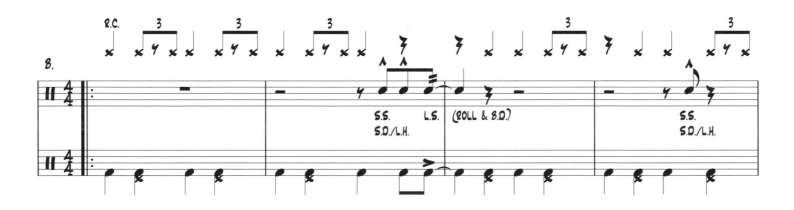

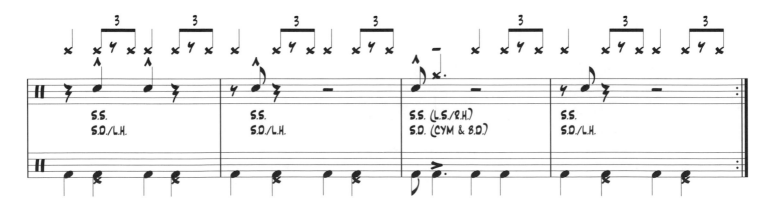

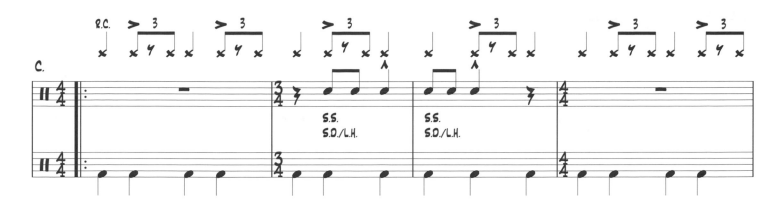

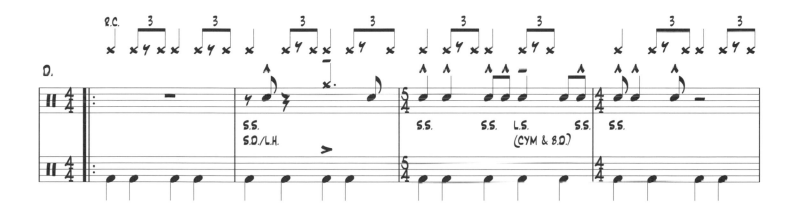

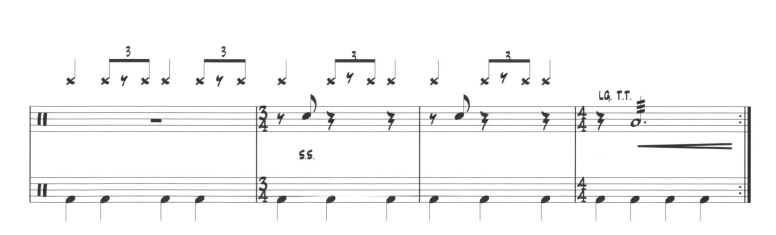

Sightreading Exercise #2

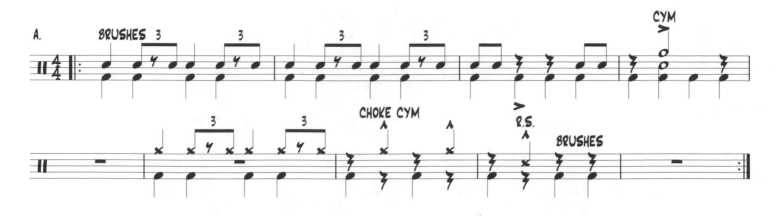

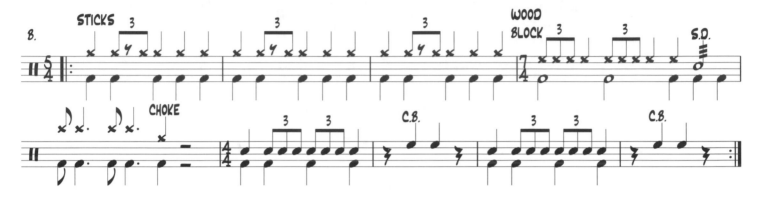

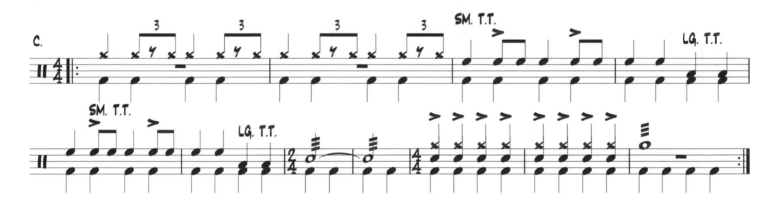

Sightreading Exercise #3

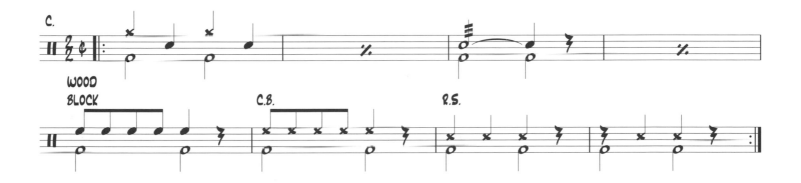

Sightreading Exercise #4

This is the first of three horn parts we have included for your sightreading practice. Where the melodic figures are marked "tacit," continue playing time and get set for the next figure.

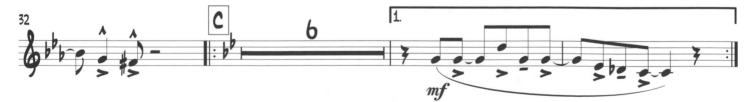

Sightreading Exercise #5

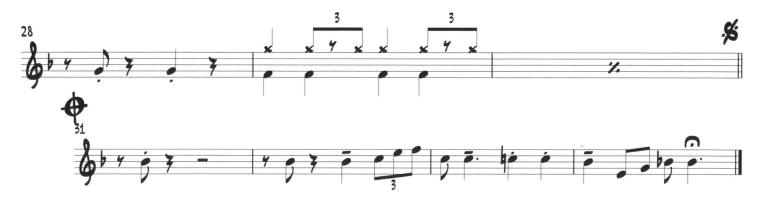

Sightreading Exercise #6

CONDUCTING PATTERNS

It is essential for drummers playing shows to understand the conducting patterns of various time signatures. Both the conductor and the drummer must firmly establish the "one" (the downbeat) of every measure in all time signatures. Without the definitive and accurate placement of this downbeat, the other beats of the measure cannot be slotted properly. The conductor can prepare and place the downbeat properly, but it is the drummer who has the power and equipment to move and settle the band in the various tempo changes.

The following illustrations show the conducting patterns with the conductor **facing the orchestra** (in other words, from the player's viewpoint).

4/4 Time

On each numbered beat, the conductor will return to the center spot (the dot) and move to the next beat of the measure. Conductors may take liberties and have various movements around the pattern, but there must not be any confusion about where "one" is placed.

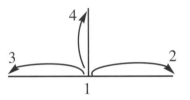

3/4 Time

Again, the dot becomes the center, or crossover spot for the pattern.

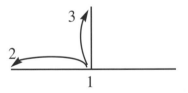

Fast 3/4 in "One"

Because the tempo is moving rapidly, a definitive "one" (downbeat) becomes even more critical. Beats 2 and 3 are within the upward motion of the conductor's pattern.

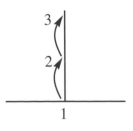

2/4 Time

Like the fast 3/4 time in "one," the 2/4 conducting patterns moves down and up.

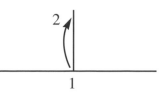

2/2 (Cut) Time

A great deal of show music is written in cut time. The conducting pattern is like 2/4, but remember that in cut time a half note gets one beat (as opposed to 4/4, where the quarter note gets one beat).

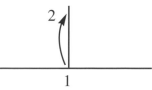

6/8 Time

This is basically a "two" pattern. However, at a slow tempo this pattern can be a bit confusing until you analyze it. Keep in mind the imaginary spot (the dot) in the center of the pattern; this will help you understand the flow of the conducting motion. At a fast tempo, this pattern is conducted in "two." But at the same time, you must be thinking and counting six beats to the measure in order to play the proper subdivision of the rhythmic patterns.

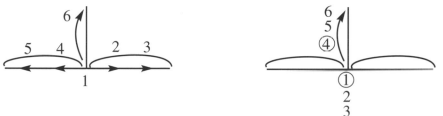

12/8 Time

This pattern presents the same initial confusion as the 6/8 pattern. The conducting motion is basically a 4/4 pattern, but you must be thinking and counting twelve beats to a measure to play the proper rhythmic subdivisions. Eventually you will internalize the counting of the numbers.

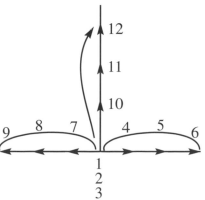

PERSONAL OBLIGATIONS

A truly dedicated, professional musician possesses the combination of musical skills and the cooperative attitude to make every performance a successful one. He or she must be cognizant of the goal, which is to play the performer's music as effectively as possible and assist in every way to resolve any problems.

The conductor usually has a two-hour rehearsal to prepare all the music for the show. This is not a lot of time, especially if the music is difficult. The rehearsal can be most productive when all the musicians, and especially you (the drummer) conform to the following:

Punctuality

Out of all the ensemble members, you have the most equipment to set up, so allow as much time as necessary to be ready for the downbeat.

Concentration

Complete and focused attention is absolutely necessary. When the conductor has to repeat instructions, valuable time is lost. However, this should not be a deterrent for any questions of clarification you might have; all questions should reference the location in the music and the problem you need resolved.

Equipment

In addition to the regular drum kit, you should try to know what additional accessories might be necessary. Always have a couple pencils—including a red one—to mark and highlight any significant musical notations on your part. Consider using two music stands for any parts that may have four pages or more. Have several pairs of sticks, mallets, and brushes placed within easy access for quick changes.

Pride and Confidence

These two qualities are vital as part of your psyche to support your skills. It is important to know, however, that there is a fine line between these admirable qualities and personal ego, which can be the single most damaging personal trait to your career. Once this mental attitude has a grip on your personality, it tends to distort your sense of reasoning and reality. Don't let your previous accomplishments and accolades interfere with what must be done for the show or act you are now playing. Your personal evaluation of the music and/or the conductor's ability is irrelevant; the situation is what it is, and you can't change it. You must cope with the circumstances and make every effort to help the performance be successful. You must show how truly professional you are by helping to correct any problems; everyone will respect you for turning a difficult situation into a successful one!

In conclusion, always be ready to implement the following:

Punctuality	Concentration	Equipment Needs
Courtesy	Cooperation	Pride and Confidence

PLAYING THE SHOW

This section of the book will deal with the kind of music and acts that you might encounter when playing a show. Before each tune on the accompanying CD, Ed explains the various techniques and equipment utilized in that particular situation.

There are two charts for each tune:

1. The typical chart you would receive from the conductor

2. The revisions Ed makes to highlight all the important changes to be observed (repeats, tempo changes, etc.). These larger, highlighted markings will help to eliminate any surprises as you read the chart.

Suggestions for Practicing:

*   Read the introduction to the act before starting to listen

*   Listen to Ed's instruction on the CD for the playing approach to each act

*   Listen to the respective cut and follow the part

For each tune, examine the original part. Notice the importance of Ed's highlighted parts and how they facilitate easy sightreading of the part. Play along with each track four times per practice session.

I. MC PLAY-ON

The master of ceremonies (MC) greets the audience and introduces the various acts. The following short tune, "Whose Blues," accompanies the MC's appearance and the segue into the next segment of the show.

Track 3

Playing the Act: Ed explains the importance and usefulness of knowing how to play the hi-hats. He demonstrates several approaches.

Track 4 WHOSE BLUES
BY RICHARD DE ROSA

Conductor's Chart

DRUM SET

WHOSE BLUES

Ed's Revisions

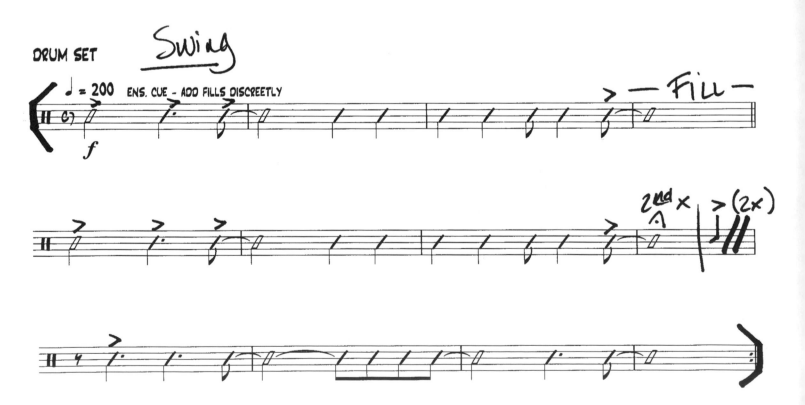

II. LINE OF DANCERS

The first act is a group of female dancers doing precision dance moves like the Radio City Rockettes. The accompanying tune, "Avalon," is in a fast 2/2 (cut time) tempo with a stop-time section for the dancers' special routine. For the finale, the tempo is slowed down for the usual high-kicking precision routine.

After the main piece, the "Avalon" refrain (track 7) is for the dancers' bows and departure.

Track 5

Playing the Act: Ed explains the correct cymbal beat for these fast tempos and the strong accent on the snare drum with the left hand on beats 2 and 4 of each measure. The stop-time section is very common in this type of act; keeping an eye on the conductor will help in the placement of the written figures in this example.

AVALON

Track 6

Conductor's Chart

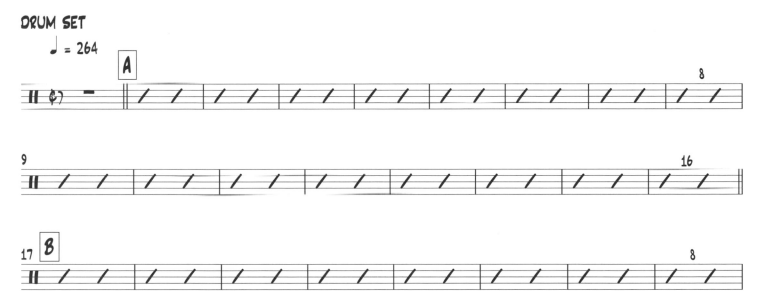

Bows: "Avalon"

Track 7

III. DANNY BOY

This slot is usually for a lesser-known vocalist who is building his/her reputation. Our chart is instrumental.

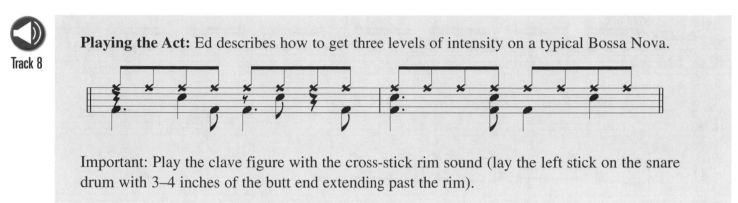

Playing the Act: Ed describes how to get three levels of intensity on a typical Bossa Nova.

Important: Play the clave figure with the cross-stick rim sound (lay the left stick on the snare drum with 3–4 inches of the butt end extending past the rim).

This is a slow Bossa Nova with a double-time feel—the melody is in a slow 4/4, but the rhythm plays a double-time figure: (See page 48 for accurate notation and added intro.)

Conductor's Chart

Danny Boy

IV. THE COMEDIAN

This is the slot where the producers want to incorporate some humor and variety. The next act is a French comedian, thus the choice of the tune "Frere Jacques."

Track 10

Playing the Act: Ed plays and explains this as one of several types of shuffle beats. The right hand plays the basic ride cymbal figure and the left hand plays the following eighth-note figure on the snare drum with accents on beats 2 and 4:

V. THE COMEDIAN'S IMITATIONS

Track 12

Playing the Act: This chart supplies a musical cushion for the act and does not distract from the artist's routine. The light, accented shuffle beat with brushes on the snare works well. Notice the bass drum figure ♩ ♪ ♪ — , which supports the horns.

Important: Switch to sticks for the "Frere Jacques" bows (track 14).

Conductor's Chart

Track 13 **SHADOWS** BY CLEM DE ROSA

DRUM SET

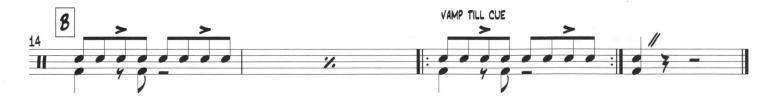

Ed's Revisions

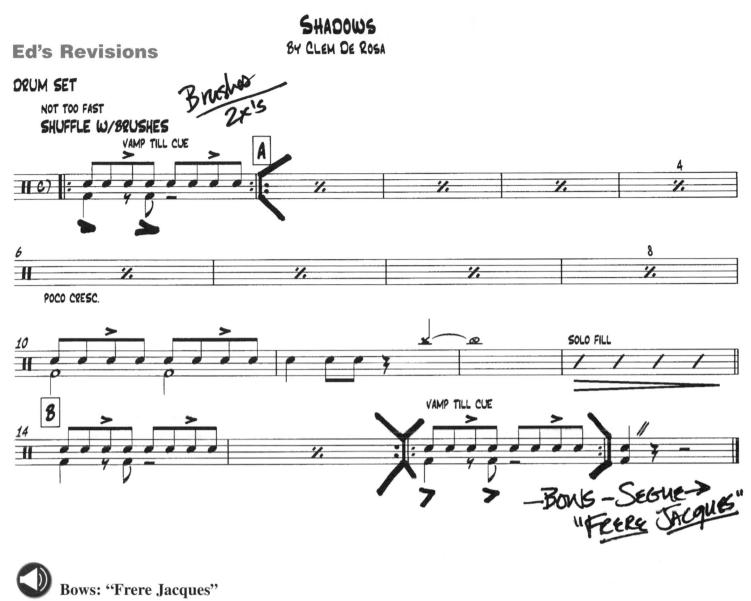

Bows: "Frere Jacques"
Track 14

VI. THE DANCE TEAM

There is no talk before this act. This happens frequently in a show, and you must be prepared for the conductor's downbeat. The show picks up at this point with a dance team doing various styles of ballroom dancing. We'll go through them one at a time.

Dance Style #1: Swing   Tune: "Oh, Marie"

Playing the Act: This is a fast shuffle. The right hand plays the basic ride cymbal figure, while the left hand plays the following figure on the snare:

Notice that the left-hand figure leaves out the first eighth note of each group of four. This is easier to play at this tempo and still captures the shuffle feel. Ed explains other shuffle approaches on the CD.

Important: Note the tempo change (slower) into the Cha Cha.

Oh, Marie

Conductor's Chart

DRUM SET

DIMINUENDO AL FINE

Oh, Marie

Conductor's Chart

Track 15
(cont'd)

STOP AND GO
BY CLEM DE ROSA

Ed's Revisions

STOP AND GO
BY CLEM DE ROSA

Count off Waltz

V.S. WALTZ

Bones pick up on (3)
GET TRIANGLE Ready

Track 16

Playing the Act: The right hand playing straight quarter notes on the cowbell ♩ ♩ ♩ ♩ locks in the time and the Latin feel. The left hand plays the conga drum figure between the snare (with snares turned off) and the small tom-tom—or the small and large tom toms.

Important: Prepare for the waltz count-off; get the triangle ready!

Track 17

Playing the Act: Dance teams use a variety of acrobatic moves at these tempos, and the music and the tempo must adjust to capture the movement. Usually rolls on the snare, tom-tom, or cymbals (Ed plays them on the cymbals with brush handles) will emphasize the move. The drummer must remain totally focused on the conductor and the act.

Important: Prepare for the tango count-off.

 **FASCINATION**

Track 18

Conductor's Chart

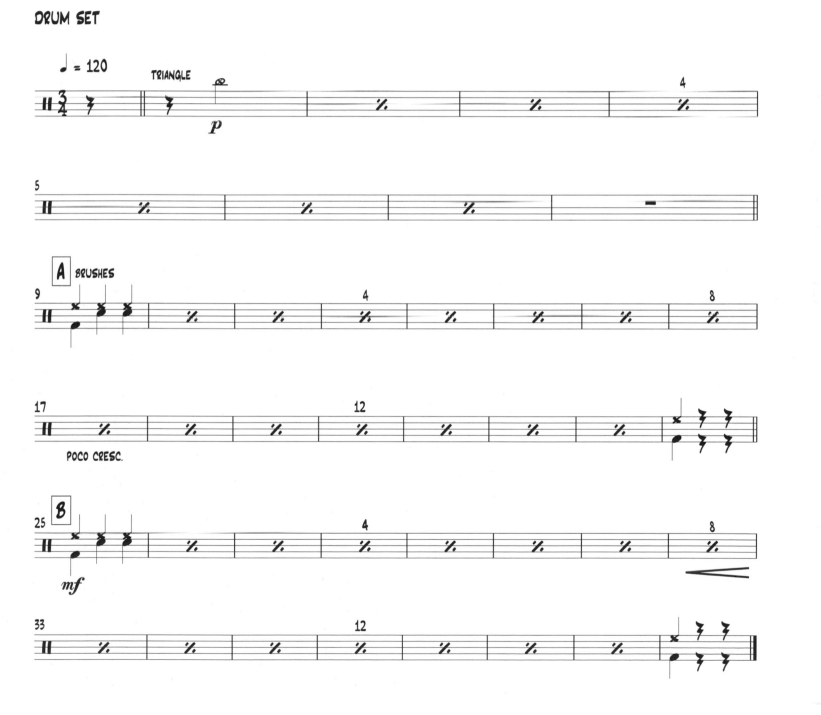

Ed's Revisions

DRUM SET

Playing the Act: This particular tune fits the tango style of dancing for this act. Notice the short sounds with sticks on the snare (with snares off) and the strong accent on the roll ♩ ♩ ♩ ♪♪♪ ♩ ♩ ♪ with the support of the bass drum.

Important: Prepare for the bolero count-off and the two-measure drum intro.

Track 20

Playing the Act: Latin drummers usually play this right-hand figure: on the side of the timbale, with some variations . The clave would be played by another percussionist, but you don't have that luxury! You must play the clave (the most important part) with the left-hand stick across the rim: Notice that the bolero clave is different from the Bossa Nova. The bass drum is played as follows:

Important: Prepare for the direct change into the rock tune.

Conductor's Chart

FIFTH SYM THEME

Track 21

> **Playing the Act:** Keep the changing rhythmic pattern simple, so the transition will be easy for the band and dancers. Once the tempo is locked in, there are many variations you can play, but remember that you are playing for the dancers.
>
> Important: Prepare for the direct change into "Whose Blues" for the dance team's bows and exit.

Conductor's Chart

Track 21 (cont'd)

FANCY FUNK
BY CLEM DE ROSA

FANCY FUNK
BY CLEM DE ROSA

Ed's Revisions

Bows: "Whose Blues"

Track 22-23

VII. THE MAGICIAN

Every variety show has a magician, whose music is light in texture and performed quietly while he/she startles the audience with magic tricks. The drummer must catch all tricks with various rolls and accessories ("toys") to enhance the act. The chosen tune here is a Viennese Waltz, "Tales from the Vienna Woods."

Track 24

Playing the Act: These waltzes are written in 3/4 time and always played at a fast tempo. They are conducted and counted in "one" with a slight accent on the downbeat. (1, 2, 3...)

The music is soft background for the magician's act. The drummer's task is to catch and emphasize the performer's tricks with rolls, cymbal crashes, and any appropriate "toys." Since magicians usually do their tricks out of tempo, it is important to keep the tempo steady with your feet and catch the tricks with your hands. (Ed discusses this on the CD.)

Track 25

Conductor's Chart

Ed's Revisions

DRUM SET

 Bows: "Tales from the Vienna Woods"

Track 26

VIII. THE TAP DANCER

As opposed to most music for tap dancers (which is usually loud and fast), our concept was music for dancers like the great Bill Robinson or Gene Kelly. They were primarily soft-shoe dancers and great improvisers—thus the choice of a softer, swinging tune with a jazz feel: "Basie Talk."

Track 27

Playing the Act: This is a good example of the importance of always locking in with the bass. The chart is an easy, swinging Basie style, loose and relaxed, but still maintains energy and intensity. The bass drum is played lightly (felt but not heard). Listen to the increase of intensity behind the piano solo—without an increase in volume.

BASIE TALK
Track 28 BY CLEM DE ROSA

Conductor's Chart

DRUM SET

Basie Talk
By Clem De Rosa

Ed's Revisions

DRUM SET

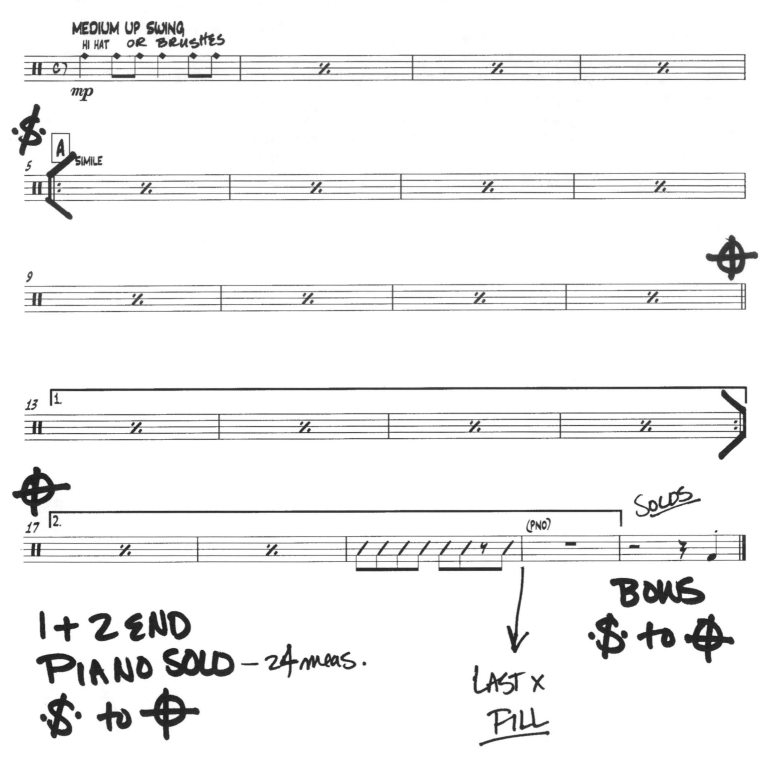

1 + 2 END
PIANO SOLO — 24 meas.
:$: to ⊕

LAST x
FILL

BONS
:$: to ⊕

IX. COUNTRY AND WESTERN

No variety show would be complete without some country and western music. This tune ("Red River Valley") was the only one not scored for the big band—just synth and drums. You'll be playing this one "blind," with no chart. Richard De Rosa (Clem's son) recorded the track for us via MIDI and captured the country-western flavor beautifully.

Track 29

Playing the Act: Ed's suggestions for playing country and western music:

1. Two sticks: One on the closed hi-hat and the other playing the "click" with the butt end on the rim. Remember you can play the butt end of the stick on the edge of the hi-hats for a fuller sound:

2. Play one stick on the "click" backbeats and one brush on the snare playing quarter notes with an accent on beats 2 and 4. The foot hi-hat plays on 2 and 4:

3. Two brushes (the quiet sound): The right hand plays four quarter notes; the left plays a short "swish:"

4. Dowel sticks ("hot rods" or "blastix"): This invention by a clever drummer really meets the need for a middle volume level between sticks and brushes. Use one on closed hi-hats and one for backbeats on the snare.

5. The "train effect" (generally for fast tunes): This hand-to-hand pattern can be played with two brushes, two dowel sticks, or two regular sticks on the snare drum. A good, strong backbeat is essential. The goal is to create a swinging feel.

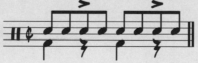

Red River Valley

Track 30

X. THE JAZZ BALLET

A recent addition to these types of shows has been the jazz ballet. World-renowned choreographers Martha Graham and Anna Sokolow are widely recognized as pioneers in this field.

Track 31

Playing the Act: The jazz waltz is written in 3/4 but is usually felt and played in "one." The basic ride cymbal figure is played in three  and the bass drum and hi-hats are played as follows:

To increase the intensity and energy, the bass will play in three; you should lock in with it like this:

WALKIN WALTZ
BY CLEM DE ROSA

Track 32

Conductor's Chart

DRUM SET

Walkin Waltz
By Clem De Rosa

Ed's Revisions

DRUM SET

PLAY TIME

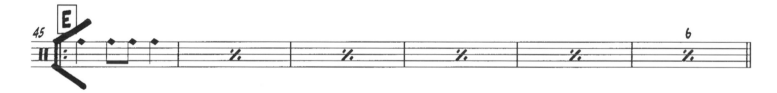

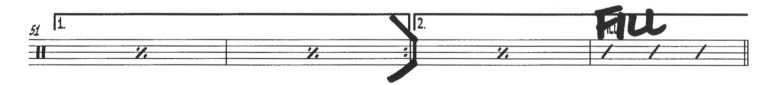

XI. THE FANFARE

This is the slot for the featured artist or main attraction.

 Track 33

Playing the Act: You must attempt to duplicate the strong sound of a large tympani. The most frequently used substitute is the large tom-tom (16" x 16"), played with the butts of the sticks or hard felt mallets. The initial attack must be strong (*ff*) and maintained until the conductor's cut-off.

Conductor's Chart

 Track 34   FANFARE

DRUM SET

Ed's Revisions

FANFARE

DRUM SET

 Track 35

CONCLUSION

The realm of show drumming involves many different aspects and we hope that this book has given you some insights as you continue along the learning path. The most important knowledge however, can only be gained through experience and good, old-fashioned hard work. So we ask again, "Drummers, are you ready?" Best of luck to you and remember to practice, practice, practice!

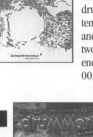